Science and Technology
Food Technology

Neil Morris

Ⓡ www.raintreepublishers.co.uk
Visit our website to find out more information about Raintree books.

To order:
☎ Phone 0845 6044371
🖹 Fax +44 (0) 1865 312263
🖾 Email myorders@raintreepublishers.co.uk

Customers from outside the UK please telephone +44 1865 312262

Raintree is an imprint of Capstone Global Library Limited, a company incorporated in England and Wales having its registered office at 7 Pilgrim Street, London, EC4V 6LB – Registered company number: 6695582

Text © Capstone Global Library Limited 2012
First published in hardback in 2012
Paperback edition first published in 2013
The moral rights of the proprietor have been asserted.

Edited by Andrew Farrow and Diyan Leake
Designed by Victoria Allen
Original illustrations © Capstone Global Library Ltd 2011
Illustrated by Oxford Designers & Ilustrators
Picture research by Elizabeth Alexander
Originated by Capstone Global Library Ltd
Printed and bound in China by CTPS

ISBN 978 1 406 22842 7 (hardback)
15 14 13 12 11
10 9 8 7 6 5 4 3 2 1

ISBN 978 1 406 22852 6 (paperback)
16 15 14 13 12
10 9 8 7 6 5 4 3 2 1

British Library Cataloguing in Publication Data
Morris, Neil.
   Science and technology: Food technology. -- (Sci-hi)
   664-dc22
A full catalogue record for this book is available from the British Library.

Acknowledgements
The author and publishers are grateful to the following for permission to reproduce copyright material: Alamy pp. **12** (© H. Mark Weidman Photography), **14** (© Spazio Foto Mereghetti), **16** (© Marco Regalia), **24** (© Phototake Inc.), **26** (© keith morris), **29** (© Neil Setchfield), **32** (© Image Source), **36** (© David R. Frazier Photolibrary, Inc.), **38** (© BlueMoon Stock); Corbis pp. **6** (© Peet Simard), **17** (© Ed Darack/Science Faction), **19** top (© Peter Ginter/Science Faction), **28** (© Envision), **40** (© Danny Lehman); Corbis Sygma p. **31** (© Pitchal Frederic); Getty Images pp. **10** (Michael Rosenfeld/ Stone), **19** bottom (Gary Ombler/ Dorling Kindersley), **25** (Nick White/Photodisc); NASA p. **15**; Photolibrary pp. **5** (Javier Larrea), **27** (Huw Jones); Science Photo Library pp. **9** (Thierry Berrod, Mona Lisa Production); Shutterstock **contents page** top (© Roman Sigaev), **contents page** bottom (© Wire_man), pp. **4** (© VR Photos), **8** (© Borodaev), **11** (© jordache), **30** (© Nayashkova Olga), **20** (© Golden Pixels LLC), **21** (© Joe Gough), **23** (© Bragin Alexey), **22** (© Thomas Zobl), **34** (© Kharidehal Abhirama Ashwin), **35** bottom (© VIPDesignUSA), **39** (© Goodluz), **13** (© Roman Sigaev), **35** top (© Wire_man), **all background and design features**.

Main cover photograph of packaging cold cuts reproduced with permission of Corbis (© Russ Schleipman); inset cover photograph of soft drink bubble reproduced with permission of shutterstock (© 2jenn).

The publisher would like to thank literary consultant Nancy Harris and content consultant Suzy Gazlay for their assistance in the preparation of this book.

Every effort has been made to contact copyright holders of material reproduced in this book. Any omissions will be rectified in subsequent printings if notice is given to the publisher.

Contents

Some words are shown in bold, **like this**. These words are explained in the glossary. You will find important information and definitions underlined, <u>like this</u>.

What are vitamins?

Turn to page 8 to find out!

When were ring-pulls first used?

Find out on page 35!

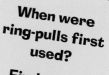

WHHT IS FOUD?

Food gives us the **energy** we need for everything we do. We cannot live without food. It helps us think, work, and run around. Eating the right amount of good food keeps us healthy. In food technology, we study how good food products are made. There are many processes involved. We find out how people grow, process, package, and sell food products. We also learn how to prepare and cook food that is healthy, safe, and good to eat.

Knowledge of food technology helps these cooks produce safe, healthy meals in their restaurant.

THE SCIENCE OF FOOD

In the kitchen, cooks put **ingredients** (parts of the mixture) together to make tasty dishes and meals. In the **laboratory** (a place where scientists work), food scientists combine their ingredients to make products for people to buy. Cooks and scientists are all involved in food technology.

LOUIS PASTEUR (1822–1895)

In 1864 the French scientist Louis Pasteur discovered that heat destroys the **bacteria** (tiny living things) that make food and drink go off. This was successful early food technology. Today, milk is still made safer by heating it to 72 degrees Celsius (°C), or 162 degrees Fahrenheit (°F), for 15 seconds. The heating is called pasteurization, after Pasteur.

MEASURING FOOD ENERGY

We measure the energy we get from food in units called **calories**. People trying to lose weight often see calories as a bad thing. But we all need calories every day – just not too many of them. One calorie is a tiny amount of energy, so scientists count in thousands of calories, called **kilocalories (kcal)**. But to confuse things, most people call these bigger units "calories". Food scientists also use a unit called a **kilojoule (kJ)**, which is about the same amount as one quarter of a kilocalorie.

Nutrients

The natural chemicals in food that help us live are called **nutrients**. The nutrients that we need in large amounts are called **macronutrients**. The nutrients that we need in much smaller amounts are called **micronutrients**. **Carbohydrates**, **proteins**, and **fats** make up the macronutrients.

Simple sugars and complex starches

Carbohydrates form our most important source of energy. There are two main types of carbohydrate. They are called simple sugars and complex starches. These are changed into a substance called **glucose** when we eat them. Glucose provides us with energy.

Food scientists divide sugars into these main groups:

- *Glucose* – in fruits and honey
- *Fructose* – in fruits and vegetables
- *Lactose* – in milk and dairy products
- *Sucrose* – in sugar beet and sugar cane, which is used to make table sugar.

Starches are made up of glucose units joined together. They are found in cereals (such as maize, rice, wheat, and seeds) and potatoes.

The flour in bread is made by grinding the grains (or seeds) of cereals such as wheat.

WHICH MACRONUTRIENTS ARE IN THE FOOD WE EAT?

	Carbohydrate	Protein	Fat
Apple	100 %	0 %	0 %
Brown rice	81 %	10 %	9 %
Chicken breast	0 %	73 %	27 %
Eggs	1 %	38 %	61 %
Lentils	67 %	30 %	3 %
Wholemeal bread	74 %	12 %	14 %

Bodybuilders

Protein helps the body grow and repair itself. There are lots of proteins in:

- *Red meat*, such as beef, lamb, and pork
- *Poultry*, such as chicken
- *Fish*
- *Pulses, nuts, and seeds*.

Good and bad fats

Fats are a concentrated source of energy that also help the body absorb vitamins. People tend to think that fats are bad for them. That is because the types called **saturated fats** found in meat can increase the risk of developing heart disease. But **unsaturated fats**, such as vegetable oils, can be called 'good' fats. Experts think that chemicals called fatty acids in oily fish help reduce the risk of heart disease.

VITAMINS

Vitamins are micronutrients. They are chemicals that help us live and grow. Vitamins are usually known by letter codes rather than their scientific names. Our bodies can't store some vitamins, such as vitamin B and vitamin C. We need a constant supply of these vitamins from the food we eat.

Fruits are a good source of vitamins and other nutrients. Large markets offer many different kinds of fruit, depending on the season.

Vitamin	Chemical name	Good food sources
A	Retinol	Carrots, dairy products
B_1	Thiamin	Nuts, vegetables, whole grains
B_9	Folic acid	Fruit, leafy green vegetables
B_{12}	Cobalamin	Eggs, fish, meat, poultry
C	Ascorbic acid	Citrus fruit, broccoli
D	Calciferol	Margarine, oily fish

Minerals

We also need traces (tiny quantities) of about 15 minerals, which are found naturally in the ground. Essential minerals are calcium, iron, magnesium, phosphorus, potassium, sodium, and sulphur.

Food groups

We can put foods into five main groups:

- *Bread, cereal grains, and potatoes*. These starchy foods are full of carbohydrates and fibre. They should make up about one-third of the food we eat.

- *Fruit and vegetables*. These contain carbohydrates, vitamins, and fibre. We should eat at least five portions every day.

- *Milk and dairy products*. These are a good source of protein, vitamins, and calcium. We should eat moderate amounts.

- *Meat, fish, beans, nuts, and pulses*. These contain lots of protein. Most people get as much protein as they need from eating a normal diet.

- *Fats and sugar*. These include oils, biscuits, cakes, crisps, and fizzy drinks. We need to eat some good fats, but we should not eat too many bad fats or sugary foods.

FLAVOUROLOGY

Would you like to be a flavour scientist (known as a flavourologist)? You would get to taste a lot of different foods. The job involves testing out how different food chemicals mix with each other. For example, proteins, carbohydrates, and fats react differently with chemicals that give flavour or aroma (smell). So scientists work hard to find ways of making low-fat foods as flavoursome as higher-fat varieties.

FOOD PRODUCTION

Food companies produce food in a complex process that has many different stages. It begins with growing crops and rearing animals to provide high-quality ingredients. The next stage is the manufacturing process, and the packaged products are then transported to **sales outlets** (shops), such as supermarkets.

Food-making processes

There are three different production processes:

- *One-off production*, for a single product. This is usually for a luxury food item such as a cake.
- *Batch production*, making a set number of the same product.
- *Continuous-flow production*, a form of mass production that goes on non-stop.

Bakery workers check the bread as it comes out of the oven.

In this process, tarts are filled with jam as they pass underneath nozzles.

DIFFERENT PROCESSES FOR DIFFERENT PRODUCTS

Here are some examples of foods produced by the different systems. Can you think of some more?

• *One-off* cakes, especially for birthdays. This is something you could design yourself. Individual birthday boys and girls might have special wishes for shape, size, and ingredients.

• *Batches* of bread, with different kinds of loaf baked in each batch.

• *Continuous* production of big-selling products, including baked beans and frozen pizza (see page 30).

CAD AND CAM

• Computer-aided design (CAD) allows food designers and manufacturers to test packages and products before spending a lot of money mass-producing them.

• Computer-aided manufacture (CAM) allows manufacturers to control and check every stage of the manufacturing process. They can check quantities of ingredients, conveyor belt speeds, and oven temperatures. Large bakeries use one basic CAM system to produce different types of bread. The computer changes the amount of ingredients for each batch.

Industrial equipment

Large-scale food manufacturing equipment is similar to ordinary kitchen utensils, but much bigger and stronger.

Equipment	Use
Centrifuge	Spins ingredients to separate liquids from solids
Deck oven	Contains heated chambers, one above the other, each separately controlled
Depositor	Funnel, nozzle, or tube that fills containers with a measured amount
Hopper	Large funnel-shaped container used for dispensing ingredients
Mandolin	Slices ingredients thinly and evenly
Mixer	Floor-standing machine for mixing large quantities of ingredients
Tunnel oven	A connected series of heated chambers that a conveyor belt carries food through
Vat	Large container for storing and cooking

This mixer machine helps to make smooth chocolate in a large vat.

RECYCLING PROCESS

When foods such as biscuits and pizzas are shaped, some of the dough is cut off. These pieces, known as off-cuts, are collected and added to the original mixture at the beginning of the cycle. This saves a great deal of product waste.

Watery production

Food production uses up enormous amounts of a precious resource – water. It takes these amounts of water to produce these foods:

To make ...	... the water needed is:
1 slice of bread from a standard size loaf	40 litres (70 pints)
1 x 50 gram (1⅘ ounce) bag of crisps*	46 litres (80 pints)
1 can of cola	200 litres (360 pints)
1 kilogram (35 ounces) of cheese	5,000 litres (8,800 pints)

* The original potatoes are 80 per cent water. After using all that water, mainly for washing the potatoes, the fried and dried crisps have a water content of just 2 per cent.

WHAT'S THE FIZZ IN A FIZZY DRINK?

The fizz in a fizzy drink is bubbles of gas. If you open a screw-top bottle slowly and carefully, you will see the bubbles rush to the surface. The gas is called **carbon dioxide**, and it's the same as the gas we breathe out. **Manufacturers (people who make the products)** put the gas into the drink under pressure when they bottle it. The gas dissolves into the liquid. When you open the bottle, the pressure is released and the carbon dioxide turns back into gas. This bubbles up and makes a hissing sound as it reaches the air.

QUALITY CONTROL

Food manufacturers have to make sure that their products are of high quality. <u>Shoppers will only buy from companies if they think their food is safe.</u> So it is important for manufacturers to have an effective control system which carefully checks their own procedures. Some of the quality checks are controlled by computer.

This cheese-maker is tapping a cheese with a hammer. He can tell from the sound what the cheese is like inside.

Hazard analysis

Manufacturers use **hazard analysis** to identify potential dangers. There are three kinds of danger to food production:

- *Biological hazards*, such as harmful bacteria
- *Chemical hazards*, such as cleaning fluids or machine oil getting into food (called contamination)
- *Physical hazards*, such as pieces of glass or workers' hair entering food.

In the Hazard Analysis Critical Control Points (HACCP) system, checks are made at the points where dangers are most likely to occur. This system is very successful for quality control.

IDEAS FROM SPACE

HACCP was first used in the 1960s, when the US space agency NASA asked a company to produce safe food for its astronauts. It was vital that astronauts remained healthy, and they did not want any bits of food floating around their spaceship. So NASA asked for bite-sized foods that were free of harmful bacteria and crumbs. The food company set up the first HACCP system to make sure their space food was perfectly safe.

These people working on the International Space Station are sharing a meal in space.

STOPPING FOOD POISONING

In 1996 there was an outbreak of food poisoning in Scotland. Nearly 500 people fell ill and 17 died. The cause was found to be contamination of cooked meat caused by bacteria called *E. coli*. Following an inquiry, the HACCP system was adopted throughout the whole British food industry. The United Nations Food and Agriculture Organization agreed that it was essential to bring in a food safety system like this.

PRESERVING FOOD

In ancient times the most popular methods of preserving food (keeping it from spoiling) were drying, salting, and smoking. All these methods remove water from food to stop or slow the spread of harmful micro-organisms (tiny living things such as bacteria).

Drying fish on these wooden racks will help preserve them. The fish may be salted, too.

Traditional preserving methods

Other traditional preserving methods include:

- *Fermenting* – using **yeast** (a kind of fungus) or bacteria to produce chemicals called acids and alcohols
- *Jamming* – boiling in a sugar solution
- *Pickling* – covering food with an **acid solution**, such as vinegar.

Canning was introduced in the 1800s, for preserving meats, fruits, and vegetables. Freezing came in a century later. Freezing is effective because the low temperature in a freezer kills the micro-organisms that cause food to go bad.

Tins of peeled tomatoes pass along a production line in a canning factory.

Heat and radiation

The Ultra Heat Treatment (UHT) process heats milk to more than 135 °C (275 °F) for just one second. An unopened carton of UHT milk can last for up to six months. Another process, called **irradiation**, bombards food with a kind of light called gamma rays. These rays kill micro-organisms. If a food has undergone one of these processes, it is shown on the label.

Additives

Chemicals called **additives** are used to improve the properties of processed foods, such as:

- *Preserving* (increasing the shelf-life of the product)
- *Altering texture* (the way the food feels in the mouth), such as making food smoother
- *Improving colour, taste, or smell*.

Some people are sensitive to certain additives, so they need to know what is in their food. In most countries all additives have to be listed on food labels.

Genetic modification – yes or no?

Genetic modification (GM) means changing an animal's or a plant's **genes**. Genes are the basic units that pass characteristics, such as size and colour, from one generation to the next. GM can be used to make crops more useful. But many people who are concerned about the environment (called **environmentalists**) are against it.

Arguments for and against GM

For – GM foods could …	Against – GM foods could …
✓ build up resistance to pests	✗ spread to non-GM crops and wipe them out
✓ help the **developing world** (poorer parts of the world) by increasing harvests	✗ leave farmers in the hands of giant companies that control GM seeds
✓ lower food costs by increasing yields (the amount each plant produces)	✗ reduce biodiversity (the world's wide range of plants and animals)
✓ benefit health by being enriched with nutrients	✗ have health risks that we'll only discover when it's too late
✓ improve taste and shelf life.	✗ have consequences that people don't know about or haven't thought of yet.

What do you think – should people produce GM foods or not? Use the arguments above to make and explain your decision.

A scientist checks the growth of food plants in a greenhouse laboratory. Genetic modification might help the plants grow faster.

Vegetarian cheese

Cheese is traditionally made using rennet, which comes from calves' stomachs. Rennet naturally separates milk into lumps. In the 1980s scientists found a way to create the substance that makes rennet work. They did this by taking genes from rennet and putting them into micro-organisms. The resulting cheese is not labelled GM, because the micro-organisms are not actually part of the cheese. And vegetarians can eat it, because it contains no animal matter. About 90 per cent of hard cheese in the UK is made this way.

If these cheese-makers do not use rennet, the cheese can be labelled as suitable for vegetarians.

Organic production

A food is labelled "organic" if it has been produced without the use of pesticides (chemicals used to kill pests, or insects) or human-made fertilizers. Environmentalists say that organic farming is much better for the land. Also, by eating organic foods, we are less likely to be eating chemicals from pesticides. But is organic food better for you? Some scientific studies show that organic food is safer and more nutritious, while others find no difference.

COOKING TECHNIQUES

Food production in the home is similar to commercial food processing. The difference is that things are done on a much smaller scale at home.

Food technology at home includes a number of processes:

- *storing raw food*
- *preparing a range of ingredients* (cutting, grinding, weighing, etc.)
- *combining ingredients*
- *shaping foods*
- *cooking and cooling*
- *storing cooked food safely and **hygienically** (cleanly).*

This cook is carefully cutting raw fish into thin slices.

ANCIENT METHODS

The ancient Greeks and Romans wrote about the way they prepared food. A rich Roman merchant named Marcus Gavius Apicius was an expert on fine food and wine during the 1st century AD. Historians believe he wrote a book of 500 Roman recipes called *De re coquinaria* ("On the Subject of Cookery"). A century later, a Greek cook called Athenaeus wrote a book on food. It follows a conversation between two men enjoying a feast.

Combining ingredients

Food scientists, chefs in restaurants, and cooks at home use the same basic ingredients to make their dishes. Ingredients react with each other in different ways, depending on their chemical make-up. Here are some of the basic combining processes.

Binding	Causing ingredients to stick together, e.g. using egg in a biscuit mixture
Enriching	Adding ingredients such as vitamins or minerals (e.g. calcium or iron) to improve the **nutritional** quality of food
Enrobing	Coating food with an ingredient, e.g. breadcrumbs
Flavouring	Adding ingredients to change flavour, e.g. herbs and spices, or sugar for sweetening
Setting	Using ingredients to make foods firm, e.g. gelatine for desserts such as jelly
Shortening	Using fats, e.g. lard or margarine, to make pastry less stretchy and more crumbly
Stabilizing	Adding ingredients, e.g. eggs and flour, to help food keep its structure.

This cod fish was coated in breadcrumbs before it was cooked.

COMMERCIAL FLAVOURING

From 1920 to 1960, bags of crisps were sold with a twist of salt. Then manufacturers found that people wanted different flavours. The first was cheese and onion. Today there are lots more. The flavour comes from powdered seasoning, which is sprayed on to the crisps just after frying. The seasoning flavours are originally made from the real food – cheese, onion, salt, vinegar, and so on.

Emulsion, foam, or gel?

There are different kinds of mixtures in cooking, depending on how ingredients react with each other:

- A *solution* is formed when one ingredient (the **solute**) dissolves in another (the **solvent**). Syrup is a solution of sugar dissolved in water.

- An *emulsion* is a mixture of two liquids that will not form a solution. The liquids (such as oil and vinegar) need a substance called an emulsifier (such as the lecithin in egg yolk) to stop them separating again.

- A *foam* forms when air mixes with a liquid (such as whipped cream or meringue)

- A *gel* is a semi-solid mixture (such as jelly). It is made of a small amount of solid (gelatine) in liquid (water).

- In a *suspension*, a solid (such as flour) is held in a liquid (such as milk). The solid does not dissolve and may sink if it is not stirred (e.g. when making a cheese sauce).

BATTERY, BARN, OR FREE-RANGE EGGS

Battery hens are kept in cages. Barn eggs are produced by hens that are kept in sheds (or "barns"), where they can roam. Free-range hens wander about a farm during the day, and at night go into hen houses. Studies have shown that free-range eggs contain more vitamin A and good fats than cheaper battery eggs. These chemicals are important for a healthy diet.

Free-range hens like these have a more natural life than battery hens.

All-round good eggs

Eggs have lots of different uses in combining ingredients and making mixtures.

Aerating
Eggs help add air – for example, to make cakes light

Thickening
They help to thicken runny foods such as custard and sauces

Binding
They help to hold food together – for example, the pieces of meat that make up burgers and meatloaves

Coating
They are used with bread to coat fish

Setting
They help foods such as lemon tart to become solid

Emulsifying
They are used to stop liquids from staying separate

Glazing
They give a shiny or coloured surface to biscuits and scones

Always cook eggs thoroughly

Raw eggs may contain *Salmonella* bacteria, which can cause serious food poisoning. Always store eggs in a refrigerator and wash your hands after handling them. Cook eggs thoroughly, so that both white and yolk are firm. It is best to avoid making mayonnaise yourself. Mayonnaise manufacturers use pasteurized eggs. They heat the eggs at a certain temperature, and the heat kills the bacteria (see page 5).

FOOD SAFETY

Everyone involved in food production must help protect health. We can all do this by using **hygienic** (clean) methods in storing, handling, and preparing food. <u>Bacteria are the main cause of food going off</u>. Given warmth, moisture, and time, these tiny micro-organisms multiply in large numbers in food and water. They cause food poisoning, which affects the stomach and makes sufferers vomit and have diarrhoea.

A powerful microscope makes these Listeria *bacteria look 3,000 times bigger than they really are.*

LISTERIOSIS OUTBREAK

In 2008 an outbreak of a disease called listeriosis caused 22 deaths and 57 cases of serious illness in Canada. *Listeria* are bacteria that cause food poisoning. The disease can make people very ill. It was traced to a food processing factory near Toronto. The *Listeria* bacteria were in packaged salami and other meat products. They may have been introduced during packaging.

Cook food thoroughly

Cooking food thoroughly destroys bacteria. Here are minimum temperatures for cooking meat. Cooks in companies, restaurants, and in the home all need to follow the same rule.

Joints/cuts of beef, veal, lamb	63 °C	145 °F
Pork, minced beef	71 °C	160 °F
Chicken and other poultry	74 °C	165 °F

Stopping the spread of bacteria

Food manufacturers keep all their machines and equipment clean, and they stick to important safety rules. Bacteria can spread from one food to another, and this can happen easily with meat.

Here are some basic safety rules to follow when handling meat:

- Store raw meat on the bottom shelf of the fridge, so that it doesn't touch or drip on to other foods.

- Wash your hands thoroughly with warm, soapy water after you have touched meat. Keep your fingernails trimmed and clean.

- Dry your hands well using a disposable kitchen towel or hand dryer.

- Wash chopping boards, knives, tongs, and other utensils in warm, soapy water as soon as possible after use.

- Don't put raw meat next to cooked food on a grill. Otherwise, bacteria could spread before they are destroyed by the heat.

Cooks should always make sure that their work surfaces and equipment are clean.

Killer bacteria

Around 5.5 million people in the UK are affected by food poisoning every year. Most of these cases are a result of eating in restaurants or cafés, or from takeaways or fast food outlets.

Using the right equipment

It's important to know how to use the right equipment for preparing and cooking food. For example, the easiest way to check that meat has been cooked through is to use a food thermometer. Most modern food thermometers give a digital read-out of the temperature when they are pushed into the meat and left for a few seconds. There is even a special kind which can be pre-set to pop up when the meat reaches the right temperature.

Electrical appliances

There are lots of electrical devices to help you prepare food efficiently and safely. Here are some of the main ones.

- *Bread machine or bread-maker* – made up of a pan, or tin, with a paddle in the middle for mixing dough. It has an oven with a control panel. It can also be used to make pizza bases.

- *Food processor* – a machine with interchangeable blades and disks, useful for liquidizing soups and making pastry.

- *Hand blender* – a hand-held device that helps you mix, whisk, chop, and blend.

- *Juicer* – a machine that extracts (takes out) juice from fruit and vegetables.

- *Microwave* – a small oven that cooks or reheats food very quickly (see next page).

This cook is using a food thermometer to check the temperature and make sure the meat is cooked.

BRIGHT IDEA: MICROWAVE

In 1945 an American engineer called Percy Spencer was working with some electronic equipment when he noticed that a chocolate bar in his pocket started to melt. He discovered that microwaves from the equipment had caused this. Two years later the company he worked for produced the world's first microwave oven.

Just a little water needs to be added to peas to cook them in a microwave oven.

Good vibrations

How does a microwave oven work? It produces **electromagnetic radiation**. This is waves of electric and magnetic energy. These high-energy microwaves cause water **molecules** (groups of atoms) in food to vibrate rapidly. The vibrations cause friction (rubbing), which produces heat, and this cooks the food.

DESIGNING A DISH

Designing a food product follows three stages:

design brief ➡ market research ➡ design specification.

The design brief explains the need for your product and who it is for. Next you need to do market research, to find out what people want from the kind of product you are designing. Then you make your design specification, which is a detailed description of the product.

Design specifications might include:

- *size, shape, and weight*
- *ingredients and quantities*
- *equipment to be used*
- *appearance, taste, and texture*
- *costs.*

You could design a delicious drink, like this raspberry and blueberry yoghurt smoothie. Then you could give it a name, such as "Double Berry Dream".

Sandwich spec

Imagine you are working for a food company. You might design a sandwich. Who is going to be interested in your sandwich – a particular age group? Where and when will it be eaten? Will you make it a rectangle, triangle, or square, or a range of all three? What kind of bread will you specify? There is a wide range of fillings to choose from. You will need to think about the cost of the ingredients, and they will need to go well together. And how will you package and store them to keep them fresh and tasty? There are so many things to consider.

Packaging

Food designers have to think carefully about how food is stored and packaged, not just its taste. A banana and chocolate sauce sandwich sounds new and fun. But the chocolate sauce might make the bread soggy, which could make the sandwich fall apart. Yuk! A star-shaped sandwich might look nice, but would be difficult, slow, and expensive to cut. And imagine trying to make a star-shaped sandwich box!

Heston Blumenthal's dish of shellfish and seaweed is called "The Sound of the Sea". You can even eat the pretend sand and sea foam while you listen to a real sea through earphones.

BACON-AND-EGG ICE CREAM!

British chef Heston Blumenthal is famous for studying the chemical processes that go on while food is cooking. He has created some amazing dishes, including bacon-and-egg ice cream. This unusual take on the English breakfast involves leaving roasted, streaky, smoked bacon in cold milk overnight. His restaurant customers and reviewers say it is delicious.

How it's made
frozen pizza

1 Flour, water, yeast, salt, olive oil, and sugar are mixed together to make the pizza base. Cornmeal may be added for flavour.

2 The mixture is kneaded for several minutes. Then the dough is left to rise.

3 A machine separates the dough into chunks.

4 The chunks are rolled into a flat sheet and given a dusting of flour.

5 Roller spikes pierce holes in the dough.

6 A cutting roller forms the dough into circles, and the next roller removes the offcuts.

7 A conveyor belt moves the pizza bases through a tunnel oven, where they bake for several minutes at more than 200 °C (390 °F).

8 Tomato sauce is brushed onto the base. Then cheese is sprinkled on.

9 A machine called an applicator adds meats and other toppings.

10 The pizzas are cooled. Then they are put in a freezer for 20 minutes. The temperature inside the freezer is −31.6 °C (−25 °F).

11 A machine covers the frozen pizzas in plastic.

12 Each frozen pizza is pushed into a cardboard box, ready to be delivered to the supermarket.

In this pizza factory, workers add the toppings by hand. They cover their hands, mouth, and hair to be hygienic.

BRIGHT IDEA: PIZZA MARGHERITA

Margherita pizza is made with mozzarella cheese, tomatoes, and basil. The ingredients are said to represent the three colours of the Italian flag (red, white, and green). The pizza was named after Margherita of Savoy, wife of King Umberto I (1844–1900). The Italian queen is said to have visited Naples in 1889 and enjoyed this particular topping.

FAST PRODUCTION

Production companies can control the speed of their machines. At their fastest, cutting and topping machines can produce 180 pizzas every minute.

APPEALING TO CONSUMERS

Manufacturers produce a wide range of foods for today's **consumers** (buyers). This gives people a large choice, from fresh fruit, vegetables, and other raw foodstuffs to ready-made meals such as lasagne in a box. These packaged meals need very little preparation by the consumer. Food can be bought at many different sales outlets, from small local grocery stores to large out-of-town supermarkets. Modern consumers demand this high level of choice and convenience.

Just like this real supermarket, the online version has a huge range of food products.

ONLINE SHOPPING

Today, you can even shop for food without leaving your home. New technology makes it easy for customers to choose products from a supermarket's internet website and pay online (over the internet) by credit or debit card. These services are particularly useful for people who find it difficult to get to the shops. Online shopping can help fight pollution by cutting the number of car journeys made by shoppers.

Sensory testing

Food manufacturers carry out tests to check that consumers are happy with their products. They do this with new products, and you could do the same with new designs that you create by asking your family and friends. Manufacturers also test existing products, to find ways of improving them and increasing sales. Sensory analysis (how something tastes, feels, smells, and looks) generally concentrates on taste and characteristics such as flavour, texture, and colour.

STAR DIAGRAM

Food manufacturers use star diagrams to see what people think of their products. They ask people to rate 8 characteristics on a scale of 1 to 5 (with 5 the highest score), and then join up the dots to see what shape it makes.

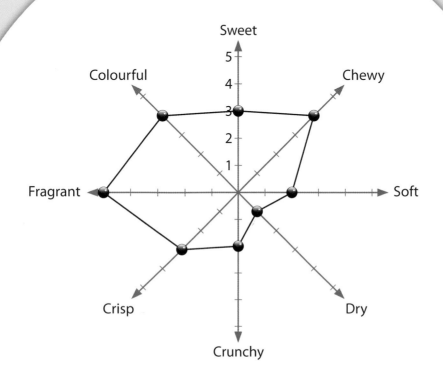

Packaging

Food packaging is used for four main purposes:

- To protect food from damage during storage, transport, and display
- To preserve food and extend its shelf life
- To describe a product
- To make it attractive to customers.

PACKAGING MATERIALS

This table shows the advantages and disadvantages of using packaging materials.

Material	Advantages	Disadvantages
Paper/cardboard	Easy to print, cheap	Easily damaged, not waterproof
Glass	Transparent	Breaks easily, heavy
Plastic	Versatile, lightweight	Not suitable for all foods
Metal	Strong, waterproof	Expensive, not suitable for all foods

Chocolate box packaging looks attractive and protects the chocolates inside from damage.

REUSING AND RECYCLING

Glass, plastic, metal, and paper can all be broken up and recycled, then reused. This saves the energy that would have been used to make new packaging. It also means that manufacturers create less pollution and use smaller amounts of raw materials (natural materials). Recyclable packaging carries symbols that show what it is made of, including the type of plastic.

TIN OPENER FACTS

Tin cans have been used for many years. But they also need to be easy to open. Early cans carried the instruction, "Cut round the top near the outer edge with a chisel and hammer."

• The first can opener went on sale in 1858, and it was really just a very strong knife.

• Can openers that used a rotating wheel to cut the metal were introduced in 1870. Their design stayed the same for a long time.

• Ring-pulls were first introduced in the 1960s, and today many cans have stay-on tabs, making it easier to recycle the whole can.

Most drinks cans are made of aluminium. This metal can be recycled, including the ring-pull.

Modified Atmosphere Packaging

Modified Atmosphere Packaging (MAP) is used to increase the shelf life of foods such as cold meats, smoked fish, cheese, fresh pasta, and salads. MAP works by changing the amounts of gases in the package when the food is wrapped in plastic. This means that bacteria grow more slowly. But some studies have suggested that MAP may remove vitamins from lettuce and other salad leaves. This means it would be less good for you.

What's on the label?

Food manufacturers have to give consumers certain information about their products. The label should include:

- The name and description of the product
- A list of ingredients, including additives (see page 17)
- Allergy information (for example, some people are allergic to peanuts and will need to know if the food contains them)
- How the product should be stored (such as in a refrigerator)
- The weight or volume of the contents
- The name and address of the manufacturer
- A "best before" and/or "use by" date
- Cooking/heating instructions
- The place of origin of the food (where it comes from).

Manufacturers and supermarkets use barcodes to keep track of products. A scanner reads the code and gives the product's price at the supermarket checkout.

CHECK IT BY PHONE

Smartphone companies have introduced "apps" (applications) for nutritional information. For example, shoppers can use their mobile phone to check the salt content of the food in supermarkets. People enter the amount of salt in every 100 grams of the food they want to buy, plus the size of the serving they want to eat. The app then tells them whether this serving has a high, medium, or low salt content.

How do scientists calculate calorie content?

If a manufacturer wants to claim that food has special nutritional or energy value, the label has to give information. This usually includes the amount of energy (in calories or kilojoules) per 100 grams (3½ ounces), or per serving. To work out this amount, scientists use a measuring device called a bomb calorimeter. <u>Calories are units of heat</u>. In the calorimeter, food is burned in a closed container (called a bomb), and the amount of heat given off is measured. Carbohydrates and proteins produce about 4 calories per gram, and fats more than twice as much (about 9 calories per gram).

TABLES OR TRAFFIC LIGHTS?

Some experts would like to see "traffic light" labels on all foods. Some supermarkets do this already. The idea is that three colours show high (red), medium (amber), and low (green) levels of the elements of food that we should try to cut down on. These are:

- *saturated fat (or "bad" fat)*
- *added sugars*
- *salt.*

The European food industry is against this system and wants to go on showing a table of guideline daily amounts (or GDAs) instead. These are the amounts of elements of foods that we should eat in a day. For example, the GDA of saturated fat for an adult is 20 grams. The GDA of salt is 6 grams.

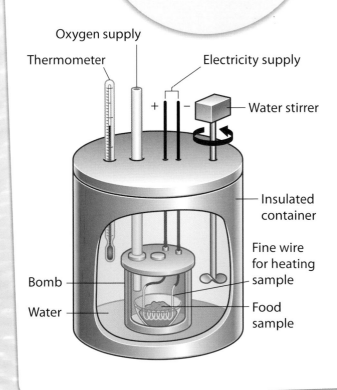

This is a diagram of a bomb calorimeter. It measure the amount of heat a food gives off when it is burned.

Oxygen supply

Thermometer

Electricity supply

Water stirrer

Insulated container

Fine wire for heating sample

Bomb

Food sample

Water

ADVERTISING

The aim of food advertising is to encourage us to buy particular types and **brands** (makes) of foods. A new brand of strawberry ice cream is more likely to be advertised than fresh strawberries. Tinned baked beans can make manufacturers more money than unpackaged green beans.

Many adverts are aimed at children and young adults, so some controls are necessary. In the UK, more than three-quarters of food advertising during children's TV programmes is for food high in fat, salt, and sugar – such as sweets, soft drinks, and crisps.

STYLING FOOD

Food stylists work with photographers to make food look attractive. They have lots of tricks. For a burger advert, for example, the stylist might improve the cooked meat by painting it with oil and brown colouring. For a flame-grilled look, the stylist might make stripes on the burger by marking it with a hot metal skewer.

Modern chefs add style to their food. Their dishes look like works of art.

Space publicity

There is a saying that "all publicity is good publicity". So is it worth advertising in space? In 2000, a pizza restaurant chain paid $1 million (nearly £620,000) to advertise on the side of a Russian Proton rocket. It blasted off, carrying a service module to the International Space Station. The following year, the pizza company worked with Russian nutritionists and delivered a vacuum-sealed, salami-topped pizza to cosmonauts aboard the Space Station.

MAKING CLAIMS

Advertisers have to be careful about any claims they make. In 2010 a large yoghurt manufacturer had to stop showing its TV commercials. This was because they said that if you ate their brand of yoghurt, you would be less likely to catch a cold or the flu. There was no real scientific evidence to back this up, so the advertisements were banned.

FOOD MILES

The distance food travels from where it is grown to where it is consumed (eaten) can be calculated in "food miles". Food is sent by aeroplane from one continent to another, and by lorry from country to country. In the United States, 15 per cent of food is **imported** (brought in) from other countries. A typical prepared meal contains ingredients from at least five other countries. All this transport uses an enormous amount of energy and causes pollution, increasing the **greenhouse effect** (warming up of the Earth).

This ship in Central America is being loaded with vegetables for dinner tables thousands of miles away.

African beans

Despite the problems, some people say food miles are a good thing. When European countries import green beans from Kenya in Africa, the food miles are high. But beans there are grown in a more environmentally friendly way than in Europe. The farms use manual labour (using people instead of diesel-driven machines) and natural fertilizer (instead of oil-based versions). They also give jobs to people in the developing world. Experts say that air-freighted beans may produce less pollution overall. This means that they do less harm to the environment.

Seasonal fruit and veg

In Europe, apples are harvested in the autumn and stored chilled for the rest of the year. This chilling uses a lot of energy. It may use more energy than transporting apples from another country, such as New Zealand. Lettuce is grown during the European winter in greenhouses or **polytunnels** that need heating and use lots of energy. It might be better for the environment to buy field-grown lettuce from countries further away.

FEEDING THE GREENHOUSE EFFECT

The atmosphere stops some of the Sun's rays from reaching Earth. Its gases also stop some heat escaping from Earth, just as glass traps warmth inside a greenhouse. Food manufacturers are adding to this natural effect by emitting (leaking out) so many waste gases from factories, planes, and lorries. Many of these so-called greenhouse gases – especially carbon dioxide – are adding to global warming.

MEASURING INGREDIENTS

Food technologists use many different measurements. Scientists weigh chemicals and other substances in metric or imperial units. For example, a test tube that measures in metric units might contain 28 grams of a chemical, which is the same as 1 ounce in imperial units.

Cooks list recipe ingredients by weight or volume. Have you noticed that different cookbooks give different measurements? That's because in Europe and elsewhere, they are usually given in metric units, sometimes with imperial equivalents. In the United States, there is a slightly different imperial system, and cooks use special cup measurements, too. The cup amounts vary for different ingredients. Here are two examples.

Volumes for liquids

Metric	Spoons	US Imperial	US cups
5 ml (millilitres)	1 teaspoon	$\frac{1}{5}$ fl oz (fluid ounces)	
10 ml	1 dessertspoon	$\frac{2}{5}$ fl oz	
15 ml	1 tablespoon	$\frac{1}{2}$ fl oz	
60 ml	4 tablespoons	2 fl oz	$\frac{1}{4}$ cup
120 ml		4 fl oz	$\frac{1}{5}$ cup
240 ml		8 fl oz	1 cup
480 ml		16 fl oz = 1 US pint	2 cups

Weights for flour

Metric	US Imperial	US cups
30 g (grams)	1 oz (ounce)	$\frac{1}{4}$ cup
75 g	3 oz	$\frac{1}{2}$ cup
150 g	5 oz	1 cup
300 g	10 oz	2 cups

Quiz

1. How long does it take to pasteurize milk at 72°C (162°F)?

a) 15 seconds

b) 15 minutes

c) 15 hours

d) 15 days

2. Which two units measure food energy?

a) grams

b) calories

c) fluid ounces

d) kilojoules

3. Which of these is not a kind of sugar?

a) lactose

b) fructose

c) sweetnose

d) glucose

4. What is the chemical name for vitamin C?

a) folic acid

b) ascorbic acid

c) acetic acid

d) formic acid

5. What is the production process for a single product?

a) batch production

b) mass production

c) continuous-flow production

d) one-off production

6. Which equipment slices food thinly?

a) mandolin

b) guitar

c) banjo

d) violin

7. Who developed frozen foods in 1929?

a) Clarence Seedorf

b) Clarence Birdseye

c) Nicolas Appert

d) Nicolas Anelka

8. When did the first can opener go on sale?

a) 1958

b) 1908

c) 1858

d) 1808

9. What does MAP stand for?

a) modified atmosphere packaging

b) mixed additional packaging

c) mild air packaging

d) mother's apple pie

10. Which instrument measures calories?

a) barometer

b) thermometer

c) odometer

d) calorimeter

Answers to the quiz

1 (a); 2 (b & d); 3 (c); 4 (b); 5 (d); 6 (a); 7 (b); 8 (c); 9 (a); 10 (d).

43

Glossary

acid solution sour-tasting liquid, such as vinegar

additives chemicals that are added to food to improve properties such as taste or texture

bacteria single-celled microscopic organisms. Some bacteria may cause illness in humans.

brand named product or group of products, usually with a trademark

calorie unit that measures energy in food

carbohydrates starches and sugars in food. Carbohydrates are converted to glucose when we eat them, and glucose provides energy.

carbon dioxide colourless gas that is produced when we breathe out and is used in fizzy drinks. Increased levels of carbon dioxide in the atmosphere add to the greenhouse effect.

consumer someone who buys goods (such as food) and uses them

conveyor belt continuous moving band that moves things along in a production process

developing world poorer countries with less technology than richer parts of the world

electromagnetic radiation electrical and magnetic energy rays, including microwaves, radio waves, and visible light

energy strength and liveliness, and their source in food; also, power that provides light and heat or works machines, including electricity

environmentalist someone who cares about and acts to protect the environment (or natural world)

fat natural greasy or oily substance found in animals and plants

gene basic unit in living things that passes characteristics from one generation to the next

glucose type of sugar in the blood that provides energy for the body

greenhouse effect warming of Earth's surface caused by pollution from waste gases that trap heat in the atmosphere

hazard analysis process to identify potential dangers

hygienic helping health and preventing disease by being clean

hygienically in a way that helps health and prevents disease; cleanly

import bring in food or other items from another country

ingredients food chemicals; substances that make up part of a food product

irradiation treating food with gamma rays to kill bacteria

laboratory place where scientists carry out experiments and research

macronutrient nutrient that we need a large amount of

manufacturer company or factory that produces finished goods, such as food products

micronutrient nutrient that we need a small amount of

molecule group of atoms (the basic particles of all matter)

nutrient substance in food that provides nourishment and helps us grow and be healthy

nutritional describing the processes of food that help us grow and be healthy

outlet *see* sales outlet

pollution damage to the natural world by harmful substances

polytunnel long plastic passage that covers plants and helps them grow

protein natural substance in food that we need for strength and growth

sales outlet shop or similar place where things are sold

saturated fat solid fat with many hydrogen atoms, such as that found in butter, hard cheese, and streaky bacon

solute substance dissolved in another substance

solvent substance in which another substance is dissolved

unsaturated fat liquid fat with few hydrogen atoms, such as that found in olive oil and other vegetable oils

yeast substance made from a fungus that is used to raise bread dough and in other food processes

Find out more

Books

Dictionary of Food and Nutrition, David A. Bender (Oxford University Press, 2009)

From DNA to GM Wheat (Chain Reactions), Sally Morgan (Heinemann Library, 2006)

Food (Eyewitness), Laura Buller (Dorling Kindersley, 2005)

Making Healthy Food Choices series, Carol Ballard and Neil Morris (Heinemann Library, 2006)

Trends in Food Technology series, Anne Barnett and Hazel King (Heinemann Library, 2008)

Websites

The Food Standards Agency focuses on food safety and hygiene:
www.food.gov.uk

Fascinating facts about the eggs we eat:
www.britegg.co.uk

Healthy eating and food safety games:
www.eatwell.gov.uk/info/games

The FoodForum website has lots of information, including an "ask the expert" feature:
www.foodforum.org.uk

Topics to investigate

There are many different topics related to food technology. The websites on page 46 might give some interesting leads. Here are some further research ideas.

Fair trading in the developing world

The Fairtrade Organization helps small farmers in poorer parts of the world by making sure they get a fair price for their produce. In 2010 there were 746 official fairtrade organizations in 58 countries, representing more than 1 million farmers and workers.

You could research how this system works. For example, cocoa farmers in Ghana, Africa sell their Fairtrade cocoa beans to Europe, where they are turned into a brand of chocolate called Divine. The group of farmers (called a co-operative) has 45,000 members, who together own a third of the Divine Chocolate companies in the UK and the United States.

Multicultural food

Look further at the question of food miles. Consider how long-distance transport affects communities. Do people in rich countries expect to be able to get foods from around the world? Do people from abroad want to eat food from the country they were brought up in? Is food an important part of culture? Do food manufacturers take this into account?

Advertising-speak

Advertisers hope to persuade buyers to choose their product rather than any other product. They use friendly, positive words to describe the products they are promoting. They include words such as *value* or *economy*, *pure* or *natural*, *light* or *lite*. Look at some food advertisements and see if you can find more terms like these. Think about their meaning and whether they help you choose which product to buy.

Index